I am AMAZIN
my smile shines brighter than
the sun when it's done raining.

I am BEAUTIFUL
I love myself and I'll sing it like a musical!

I am CREATIVE
I have so many talents to show
you what I'm made of!

I am DETERMINED
I will never give up I know it will be worth it!

I am EXCELLENT
I can be a leader of leaders
just like the president.

I am FEARLESS
I am protected and strong,
I hope that you hear this!

I am GRATEFUL
For my mom, my dad,
and my guardian angels.

I am HAPPY
I'm smiling and singing
and dancing and laughing!

I am INTELLIGENT
I am so smart my brain is bigger
than an elephant!

I am a JACK of all trades
I am good at many things, Hooray!

I am KIND
I treat others how I want to be
treated all the time.

I am LOVED
By my family, my friends, and all the above.

I am MAGICAL
I have special qualities that
makes me wonderful.

I am NICE
I like to share my toys and even my bike.

I am OUTSTANDING
I love my Life because
it's sweeter than candy!

I am PATIENT
I can wait for the things that
I want without frustration.

I am a QUICK learner
I know my ABC's and I know my colors.

I am REALLY cool!
Because I eat my fruits and
my vegetables too.

I am SMART
I know how to add numbers
and how to make art.

I am THANKFUL
For my family, friends, and my
food on the table.

I am UNIQUE
I am one of a kind and happy to be me!

I am VALUED
I know my worth how about you?

I am a WINNER
Rather im a pro, or just a beginner.

I am an X-FACTOR
I make a difference in the world and
know that I matter!

I am YELLING with joy
Because I just got a bunch of new toys.

I am ZEN.
I am calm, relaxed, and peaceful within.

Made in the USA
Middletown, DE
02 May 2023

29863279R00015